New Grass under Snow

Mary Turley-McGrath

SUMMER PALACE PRESS

First published in 2003 by

Summer Palace Press
Cladnageeragh, Kilbeg, Kilcar, County Donegal, Ireland

Printed by Nicholson & Bass Ltd.

A catalogue record for this book is available
from the British Library

ISBN   0   9544752   1   6

This book is printed on elemental chlorine-free paper

for
Jim, Joan, Ronan, Helen and Teresa
and for
my mother and father

Acknowledgments

Some of the poems in this book have previously appeared in:

Beyond the Rubicon (Covehill Press 1999), *My Native Donegal* (Rathmullan Enterprise Group 1998), *Women's Work X* (1999), *The Donegal Democrat* (1999), *Poetry Ireland Review* (2001), *Riposte* (1999-2003). Some have been recorded on a poetry CD: *Eleven Ways to Kiss the Ground* (2001).

I would like to thank the National Gallery of Ireland for the information which they supplied.

Biographical Note
Mary Turley-McGrath grew up on the Galway-Roscommon border. She graduated from Carysfort Training College and UCD and taught in Rathfarnham, County Dublin before moving to Letterkenny, County Donegal in 1974 where she now teaches English. She was awarded a MSc in Education Management from Magee College, Derry in 1997. She is a founder member of the Errigal Writers, Letterkenny and has won the Francis Ledwidge Award (Dublin) 1999, the Bridget Winter Award (Antrim) 2001, and has been runner-up in a number of competitions including the Allingham Poetry Prize (1999), Charles Macklin Award (2000) and Boyle Arts Festival Competitions 2001 and 2002. She was short listed in the Scottish International Poetry Competition, 2002 and 2003.

CONTENTS

Homecoming

14th June 1946

The poppies were all closed the year you came.
A bad summer that, one of many, but
you saw their green heads from the gate,
back from your honeymoon in Malahide.

His mother opened one for you
before crossing the threshold of a house
well tidied for her new daughter-in-law,
all the old sheets and blankets burned.

You wore your fine blue wedding coat
with tan shoes and leather bag to match,
where you'd keep rent and rates demands,
Post Office receipts and Prize Bonds.

It was the end of the bad times,
tea and sugar no longer rationed
but little fruit for baking.
That winter you could find only
cherries for the Christmas cake.

The winter snows stretched out
to March. Then you helped him
on the headland with the plough.
After the first dark furrow rose,
you both stooped down to feel
new grass under snow.

Time Trap

Perhaps it's the greying embers
or moths dashing on the window pane
that always holds me to the midnight hour.

Or is it the memory of a cigarette smell
that spread through the house like incense
as Daddy sealed his day with one John Player,
his own thanksgiving ritual?

I loved to hand him packet and box
from behind the dresser clock, or better still,
strike the match and hold it
until the cigarette glowed.
Mother never knew.

River

There were no mountains where I grew up.
Only the miracle of Mc Gann's Hill
sloped towards the sky.

No drumlins ruffled the flat fields
that forced themselves to the horizon.

The river broke the flatness,
wound like a tired snake
across the farms, dividing and joining.

It was there when we crossed
the bridge to school and again
at the furthest part of the farm
it flooded each winter.

The river was shallow at the drooping salley
where the cows drank, but black and deep
at the end of the next field.

It undercut banks and gouged an islet
where reeds and long grass waved.

Golden globes of water-lilies
were just beyond our reach.
Water-hens darted from bulrushes
to their nests safe from us all.

In summer the river quietened and shrank.
The *calla* lands bloomed into meadows
and wild flowers. We built the hay stacks
under cascades of heat and ate
lemon curd sandwiches
under the single hawthorn tree.

The fields grew green again in autumn,
marked with brown circles.

A Child's Winter

Holly on top of a golden-brown dresser
and a golden-brown press in the corner
with square sunken panels reflecting the flames
from a blazing orange timber fire.

Evening brought rows of wellington boots,
damp coats on chair-backs starting to dry,
plates of curled sausages straight from the pan
and unfurled coils of dark-brown swiss roll.

When the fat sloppy snowflakes came tumbling down
from the cloud-laden wonder of winter skies
we dreamed of squat monsters with stone eyes
and the bright manna magic of Christmas Day.

Treeman

This afternoon I thought about my father
on the way back by Crannagh Road.

He loved trees with a careful passion,
knew their names in Latin and in English
from the years he worked in Galvin's Nursery.
As a boy he planted and transplanted
until he grew too tall.

We children cared little for his lore
– *quercus robur, abies grandis* and the rest –
but knew not to strip off salley rods for swords,
or jump through laurel hedges round the garden.

He never cut down trees. The big beech
that fell in the tillage field was there for years
before I helped him with a cross-cut one October.
We sawed the bigger limbs but did not cut
the trunk. He sat there in the sunset,
fistfuls of sawdust in his freckled hands.

I watched the dust run and turn
to golden grains in the long grass.

Hook Head

After the Hook there is nothing,
no more land or islands
to tie down the feet.

The sea goes on forever.
Look straight at its
hard horizontal line.

A few bewildered boats
make pitiful battle with
the surface to survive.

The lighthouse stands aloof
in black and white bands,
its beacon not yet lit.

Sheer cliffs in layers
of dark and ashen brown
fringe the land's edge.

A sign reads, *Danger.*
Freak waves and Slippery rocks.
The obvious is always stated.

Now is the time
to cross the Rubicon,
burning ships and supplies.

There can be no regrets,
no weeping or laments
in the early evening light.

We can not go back ever.

Looking Down on Apples

Late October lies
captured in the orchard-garden
hemmed by granite walls,
their fool's gold glints
all the way down
to the roofless shed.

Below the landing window
a glass table holds
the season's spoils.
Two vessels of ripe apples,
an ivory dish piled high
and a wide black pan.

In a wire basket, transfixed
by early Sunday sun,
scores of windfalls rot
like shrunken heads.

Parallels

Michelmas Term, and I carried
your books over the glass bridge
at Westland Row to Goldsmith Hall.
Below us the street fed its travellers
into the maw of the station.
Towards the river, cranes jagged
the horizon like horns
of prehistoric monsters.

Once I thought of the city as a beast,
its low eternal moan
subsuming me as I left the train,
dragging my cases to D'Olier Street.
For you, life will be different,
safe here in your halls and rooms.
The beast will rumble round the walls,
vibrate faintly across cobblestones.

You will not confront its twists and turns,
be trapped in its lair or dragged down.
Through a microscope you'll see
the inner world of cells and watch
the double helix unwind.
You will find your way in this maze
as you found your way to air
one strange September evening.

You were my first step
into the unknown, my bid for immortality,
the manic force to be part
of the future, coded and decoded.
You will carry me with you
through new millennium years,
You, my Winter Solstice child.

Easter Exit

At nine the bells began to peal
across the town, the fields, the river,
through my open window
that blessed day.

And in the hall your luggage piled,
the big sports bag, the Nike hold-all,
while you checked the tickets,
cards and wallet.

At twelve the bells began to peal.
I opened your window wide,
stripped off crumpled navy sheets
that smelt of Calvin Klein.

No bells rang out that afternoon.
A robin flew into your room.
I felt his terror in my hands
before I set him free.

Helen's Thread

That September Saturday your cases
sat neatly in the boot, on a morning
sharp with autumn's first frost.

Your last two pairs of socks still frozen
to the line. The amber sun raised vapour.
The socks refused to thaw.

In the cold glow the sycamore dropped
black-spotted yellow leaves on the tarmac
near the door. You picked one up,

tied it to a low branch with a length
of rainbow-coloured thread. It hung,
spinning, a fraction from the ground,
a last plaything for your cat.

Now, two months on, the thread remains
damp and idling in the shortening days.
But holds fast in its fibres the blue,
green and yellow of your childhood years.

A Deeper Shade

My daughter's chatter
shortens the road.
We stop for tea and watch
through full-length windows
a wedding party in full swing.
The bride dances in an ivory dress,
narrow straps on golden shoulders.

My daughter chatters
as we sit in the alcove
on a low three-seater.
We face a high black fireplace.
She orders tea and hot chocolate
in our terracotta cave.

We leave the glow of opal shades.
The drizzle over double-begonias
dances in a million sparks
under high-powered lamps.
Down the motorway,
lights shape tents of rain.
We laugh as she tells me
Reader's Digest jokes.

Brighton 2000

All along the Pier the speakers blared
Voulez-vous coucher avec moi ce soir?
to anaemic boys and willowy girls
who stood about, sexless, between
childhood and adolescence, trying
to make up their minds.

Others screamed the fear
of their delight from the roller-coaster
across the genial skies to France.

The air spun with lights and the din
of crazy zigzag machines; under
the slatted boards the sea was dark,
and drank down every sound.

Morning Flight

For a week after you left
I woke every morning at five
to see a flock of eight white gulls
rise from the river bank,
follow the line of the water
out to sea.

It is August again
and the land weighs heavy with life,
the fields and banks hold their shape
against the gods of time.
No morning flocks come up the river
to bring you back.

Odyssey

Perhaps there was no candle
in the window after all.

Yet when I reached the elbow
of the river, its blade-like
flash beckoned me.

The house stood square
against the mid-grey sky.
I faced the bitter wind
led by the memory of a light.

No sound came from the place
but the rattling of slates
and the black door opened
to a white-washed room.

Empty, though not desolate,
it took and sheltered me
against the gales,
grateful to be used again.

Pieces of timber soon kindled
to a fire and evening deepened
to a hundred shades of grey.

In the morning I found old bulbs
ready to sprout, and melted wax
upon the window-ledge.

The Dream

The dream – a Renaissance painting
in four panels. Beyond the white arch
of the back panel was a long wooden table
and benches of simple design.

A vast oak dresser filled
the panel to the right. Its shelves
were heaped with apples, tomatoes,
cabbages, peppers and wheat.

The left panel was a vaulted bedroom,
tall windows and thin white hangings.
The white bedcover folded back
like the flap of an envelope.

Someone was lying motionless,
facing away from me.
I ran my fingers from shoulder
to warm mid-thigh; she slept naked.

I left the room by a door framed
in granite. Across the square loomed
the cathedral. My brothers had arrived
for my father's anniversary Mass.

Ice Maiden

She wanted to marry,
to make love in her own tent,
not just under the stars;
to take her place at the birth-pit.

The laws of her tribe said
that first she must slaughter
one enemy soldier, bring
a head back on her saddle.
It was the Pazyryk way.

The wise women warned her
not to go into battle,
her destiny as storyteller drawn
in tattoos on her arms.

Their nightmares foretold
she'd lie in the grave-house;
that one blow to the skull
would quench all her days.

High in the Altai, a thousand
years later, held by the permafrost,
she is the story she never told.

Sunday in the Atrium

The Gallery was nearly silent that Sunday
last Spring. We wandered at our own pace
and listened to the tour guide
on the *Convent Garden*. You were enchanted
by the white-gowned postulant. She was so intent
on some heavenly vision and seemed to be
transported out of the painting,
wanting to escape the meshes of vibrant
lilies beside her, the low dark green
branches and the tall grasses
saturated with the Breton sun.

We moved on to *The Conjuror* – a bearded
old man in a plum velvet robe and fur-edged cloak.
A star of David hung on his breast.
At his knee a girl-child kneeled,
cross-armed. Her smile was enigmatic,
other-worldly, lost in wonder. She looks
away as he points his wand to the floor
and conjures up a flurry of sepia prints
by old masters, sends them floating
up and out of the room behind them.
From the shadows his pet owl watches.

We could conjure up the soldier's thoughts
of *Lieutenant Richard Mansergh St George*
who leans against the high mausoleum
inscribed *Non Immemor*. His face
is a canvas of despair. His scabbard
hangs between him and the plinth in a garden
surrounded by trees. The background
Arcadia brings no joy; its river, sky and light

unseen by him. He feels dead. Already
he ponders on the battle that will despatch
him to his forefathers. Death is tied
to him like his sword.

We parted for a while.
I tried to unwind the Jack Yeats paintings –
the blue, white and red strands of exotic confusion.
When I found you again you had changed.
You sat in the pictureless white atrium
between the shop and closed restaurant.
White walls. White light. White sound.
You sobbed out your deepest soul-secret,
released the black pain of childhood,
a self-exorcism that shook you still
on the third day of self-knowledge.
But the truth was yours now; clear, empty,
white and empty as the atrium,
blinding us like a Resurrection.

Adonis with Violets

Silhouetted in the doorway
of a house on the Via Solaris,
he offered a tray of silk flowers

in fine porcelain pots:
white lilies, orange crocus,
purple violets, blue anemone.

I chose violets,
they were the darkest.
He smiled and disappeared
into the light.

Today, the violets deepen
against a backdrop of snow.
I remember his grey eyes.

January

A morning sky, icy blue
behind the Scots pines.
Wafer-thin clouds race, detached
like the retinas from lost eyes.
The pines hold firm, ignore the sky,
immured by moans and sighs.

Two silent trees spear the air,
their whole heads snapped off
in last year's storm.
Split trunks guard the ground
like defeated Don Quixotes
who search for fantasy at their feet.

Altered Flowers

The tulips have exploded,
flung their blood petals
on the white cloth
in orgasmic frenzy.

For days they were opening
– stigmas, anthers, full carpels –
down to the zigzag yellow line
and pitch-black velvet.

The touch of inky anther
stains powder-dust on skin,
light as a thought
in stifled, dying, perfume.

Only the Bones

Roses burn in Kosovo, red petals shrivel
in empty villages on the longest day.

A spade will turn bones to the sun.
The earth speaks through skulls.

Waiting

... before them there were no such locusts as they,
neither after them shall be such.
Exodus 10.14

Father, how will we know if the plague has come,
will we see it, smell it, taste it?
No, my son, none of these ways.
Some say it comes in the air or the wind,
is carried by crows, or floats in
when the night has no stars, only lit
by a half-moon.

Father, what if it's already here?
It may or may not be,
there's no way of knowing, but if so,
soon the flocks will be dying,
first sheep and goats, then cattle and deer
will sicken and weaken, to be left
for the vultures, dry bones in the sun.

Father, is there nothing to do but wait?
Some have gone to the tombs
of our fathers, have prayed
for the knowledge of how to escape
the next terrible torment that could wipe out
our stocks, leave all the fields desolate,
break the hearts of our old men,
send our slaves to scratch
for what roots we can live on,
to save grain for the planting.

Father, you never told me of this before.
No, my son, I hoped it would never
happen again. The last time
our village was spared
we believed we were blessed,
that our gifts were accepted
by the angry God who kept disaster
from us when others were stricken.

And is waiting the worst part?
Yes, worst of all.
The fear that fills from belly to head,
that blots out all else; dreads
the sight of one fallen creature
unable to rise, legs stiffened,
aslant in the sun.

Pain

The Red Admiral beats the glass,
craves the August sun;
brown wings laced with blue,
fan and fold; drawn by red roses,
invisible barriers blind her.

Winter Secret

The last December rose rests
in a glass perfume bottle on my table,
its cerise petals in velvet overlaps
curved like the tongues of drinking cats.

It had survived the autumn's rain,
kept its beauty shut tight
as wild geese and swans braved
the night skies south, yet it opened
in full bloom for the shortest day.

Now, it nestles a centre
of old-gold to itself.

Nexus

The orange-brown leaves
of autumn are the colour
of her hair.

I see hedges where
we peeped and called
her out to play.

The field filled with
daisies and butterflies
when she came.

See you tomorrow, meant
we could hardly wait
for another day.

She was the older sister
I never had, who took us dancing
and taught us adult lore.

I saw her on her wedding day,
veil flying in the wind,
muffling the familiar laugh.

In her coffin she
looks like someone else,
waxen, worn to nothing.

Her daughter follows
the hearse, sobbing.
Her orange-brown hair
blows in the late
October gale.

Vicus Papissa
Street of the Woman Pope

What forced her in the end?
Was it the old need that seldom
showed, but went in and in,
cutting to the core?

Why did she take the cold-hot
plunge in the dead of light,
killing cries in the dark,
dreading the chance of birth?

Was it the fear of being herself
when she saw dead leaves take off
from a path by the sea
like a flock of shocked birds?

They killed her in the street.
No Pope has walked there since.

Herons in February

A sudden snow shower sweeps the valley,
smothers the fields in a liquified sandstorm.
When it has spent itself, sun seeps through.
Two herons fly in on the storm's path,
following the drain that splits the field.

They choose their terrain near a low
hedge between clumps of rushes.
One disappears down the bank;
the other moves away and stops,
relaxes his white breast and throat,
the blue-grey wings, the underlay
of black that forms an edging.

In quiet dejection he waits,
blends with brown hummocks
and lumps of green sheen slime
left after drainage; behind him
a row of fallen fence posts.

Penelope Regrets

The shadow of his former self
lay sleeping on their bed.
Twenty years of wandering
were chiselled on his skin,
had sucked the colour from his hair,
had shallowed out his face.

Those early years, the crying child,
nights in the courtyard freezing
the loss and terror to her soul.
Screams of men and horses
beating in her head,
the crack of wheels, the bloodied spears,
the pyres of burning dead.

A night sea breeze brought sounds
of creaking masts and singing,
sails hoisted in favourable winds.

She watched the suitors jeer
a merchant with his oils and silks.
They wanted wine, they said,
to seduce the crazy queen.
Hurling his cloth across the yard,
throwing his perfumes to the dogs,
for once they all agreed
he would never get to see her.

In the dark she found the silk
scattered near the fountain,
wrapped it loosely round her,
drifted to the ghostly harbour
guided by the ripened moon.

On the sea the boats were still.
Music from the courtyard flowed.
She did not feel hours slip away,
the joy of being herself, unknown,
no greedy suitors, no lustful looks.
While pink-shelled east
spiralled to red-lipped dawn
she found again her marriage bed,
kept this secret buried in her head.

Night Music

I've been reading poems
for five nights in a row,
winding through the lines
of other people's lives, seeing
what is on the page or not
and wondering why that line stops
there or doubles back too soon.

I play the music
you gave me years ago,
a Christmas present the children
borrowed for study-time
– *it relaxes us*, they said, or,
classical music makes us intelligent –
so it's only now,
when they've all left home but one,
that I can enjoy Fauré's *Pavane*
and Mozart's *Concerto No.21*,
the *Elvira Madigan* theme.

And I remember when Elvira
practised her tightrope walk,
the balance of her body on the line
between two apple trees;
the innocence of a long white dress
against the summer's green and how
she loved to a point beyond passion,
feared neither disgrace nor death.

I recall the evening
I was late from lectures.
Turning down the last flight
of stairs, I saw you leave the hall,
and as I ran, watched you vanish
through revolving doors and scurry down
the steps before I could call
your name.

You stood tense
between the round granite pillars
and looked back at me,
your hair dark and long
falling almost to your eyes.
I touched you and said your name
again and again until you smiled.
As we walked towards
Saint Stephen's Green, we kissed.

April

Today, my first to write in natural light.
I pull the curtains fully back;
along the wall, moss mats fixed in shade
under grey-green cocoons of black willow,
a few already turned to spiky-yellow.
Behind the outcrop, gorse in a saffron blaze.
The ancient pines find new circadian rhythms.

The earth pulses, pumps new life
into this carbon-heavy world, insists
on nature's victory in rebirth, knows
forests and jungles have buried towns and temples,
volcanoes encased palaces and cities, and seas
hide the lost remains of Alexandria and Gomorrah.

Fragments

The woman on the Dublin Express
taught English in a Turkish College
near a city close to the desert.

Her students were anxious to learn
but sometimes left for their mountain
villages and never came back.

One day in the city she saw
chunks of Greek and Roman pillars
used to prop open a window.

The laws of Allah are strict, she said,
*but we need something beyond ourselves
by which to live.*

Capricorn

A late gift, you said,
my birthday two days past.
The green velvet box revealed
a silver torc on a linked chain,
silver on green in the candlelight.

As we crossed the cobbled square
rain danced under orange lights.
I stroked the torc's cool surface
next my skin, fingered
the space for the missing piece.

Interim

October frost splits the air
and seals the morning fields
with a skim of silver light.
Across the river, smoke funnels
north like a Lowry painting.

At the garden's end, leafless
whitethorn branches twist
a phantasmal tapestry studded
with crimson haws. On these
garnets two blackbirds feast
and flutter to the ground

as if they recall blackcurrants
buried in the grass, or the time,
years ago, when we sowed
a garden here. Then the children
learned the miracles of soil,
saw carrot shoots appear and
lettuce-leaves tighten into heads.

The clothes-line beside the fence
is tense with socks and towels.
The plastic pegs sting the skin,
freeze-glue the finger tips and jolt
the brain. The Indian Summer
has finished now, and the earth's
heart holds little warmth.

From the hedge I break snowberries
plump with cold sap and with them
place two branches of blue hydrangea,
their pale faces innocent as rain.
From the rose-bush I cut
the last red roses, smell the petals
damp and drugged with time.

Imaginary Lover

She had kept this day for you,
hoarded hours and minutes,
shelved the trivial chores
that soak the sap of vision.

But no knock broke
the quiet of afternoon,
just the quick phone call
that you were too busy.

Evening lurched in; birds sang;
sun switched with showers;
the black and white keys locked
silent symphonies.

She poured through every book,
slid her fingers down the tension
of their spines, but could not find
an antidote.

Falconer

And you my falcon muse
will leave me for a while,
to rest from summer's heat
and learn from what has passed.
We can not remain unchanged.
Even the scented summer rose
will not survive the snow.

The Visit

Ghost trees stood sentinel
in the headlights
that sharp December night.

The hallway light glared
through frosted glass.

My knock brought you to the door,
half-blocked by strident firethorn.

Red berries vibrated
among its spiny branches
like dilated blood globules.

I let it grow to keep you out, you laughed.
You should have known better, I said.

All Saints' Day

The group gazed back at the grotto
of the Virgen de la Peña,
three old women to the front
small and straight in black dresses and jackets,
faces tanned by time and sun,
short hair curled neatly, thin wedding bands
on their fingers, heads inclined as they talked,
with quick furtive glances – out of place
like a chorus from *Bernarda Alba*.

Their sons moved away to look down
at the rising apartments and across over Mijas
where forest fires had burned for three days
right to the edge of the town.
The men talked in relays and relaxed
their generous bellies. One lit a cigarette
and sat on the wall, his soles dangled
over the sheer drop a hundred feet below.

Their daughters drifted down the gardens
to the oval bullring. One sat
in the seat of *El Presidente* and delivered
a mock commentary to *Señores y Señoras*.
Her audience hooted and clapped. They talked
all together, their voices booming
from the wide stone terraces, round
wine walls and across the sea-sand
of the bullring floor.

But where were their grand-daughters –
the five young girls with puce
pouting lips and brave brown eyes,
in tight teeshirts that barely touched
the tops of their trousers?
Had they gone down the narrow streets
to search for shops and cyber cafés,
answering the beat of a newer world?

February

The goddess cannot enter
this place of dryers and combs
where the past is trimmed away
and lies on the wooden floor
in patches of auburn, brown and grey.

A rose tree skeleton is beaten
into the pebble-dash,
at its base the thin,
green, knife-blade daffodils.

This is my view and only this
as the light swings in and out
on the cupid of Caravaggio.

Goddess

La Concha looks down,
her peak veiled in cloud,
blind to the Saturday market
in the Plaza de Toros;
the gleam of pots in yellow and blue,
frenzied traffic under low solid palms.

La Concha looks down
in the afternoon sun, her head
the nub of a down-turned fan,
her ridges and gullies spread
like ripe carambolas,
pressing against a cloudless sky.

La Concha looks down
in the late evening glow,
where ivy trails the bullring steps.
Her sides fold in the shadows, drawing
power to herself. She closes
her shell at the fading of light.

Waterlines

I am the river bed.
You flow over me,
a seamless robe
of endless shifting shades;
opalescent, mercurial, opaque.
You bear alluvium to fields
flattened by generations of hay-makers.
These *calla* lands that stretch
west to distant bogs and the tower
of Kilmore graveyard.

I am the river bed.
Through you I glimpse
the sun in autumn.
Against its south-west glow
wigeon, teal and mallard rise
from sighing sedge
or black refracted sloping reeds.
Water-hens rummage for food
under the fallen salley,
its trunk a blackened shaft.

As autumn deepens
your currents build
and force against the banks.
They seep out where
the land has dipped,
find life in new levels
as sinuous streams.
They absorb the low grass, feed
one another and then conjoin
in a mirage of mirror glass.

Now I do not know you.
Spread across fields
you engulf acres, find
an empire of your own.
Obliterated divisions leave
a deep-silver mass, solder
fusing towards the winter sky
of endless mist and rain
broken by curlew cries
and flocks of wild geese.

When Spring days warm,
floods fold back,
the time of growth begins.
I feel your force return.
You find your course, obey
the bank's restraint, the season
of free-floods spent. Soon
water-lily pads carry green
and golden bulbs, yellow irises
crown your banks.

By the longest day
you feign forgetfulness,
drop your guard and
shrink to half your width.
I see for myself
the pure blue sky and walls
of black-mossed stones dredged
from my depths a century ago.
Part of me belongs to the land
like remnants of a lost domain.

I am the river bed.
You flow over me.
Late in summer I see myself,
a palette of gravel,
stones and sand. In this tapestry
are the atoms of my being,
minuscule woven pixels
multiplied in millions,
bedded together
by the weight of water.

Fortune-fall

Here it all is at last,
not just some, but the whole lot
in one tremendous month;
so much together when I had
almost given up, settled
into the best groove I could find,
learned to maintain dignity and
be happy with my lot.

Then the shutters pulled open
and the sun of fortune blazed in,
sent me scrambling to find notes,
papers, books that once
mapped out the journey,
gave instructions on what to do
and how to do it, contingency plans
for when storms broke or sailors rioted.

But like an ancient Mariner, my plans
becalmed, diversions and distractions
became the order of the day
and the enterprise faded, so that
I packed the books and papers,
reflecting sadly on how much
they had given me and I them;
cried that they would not be used again,
or so I thought last year.

Now I will go to the attic space,
unpack the boxes, see if maps need
updating. The journey will be the same,
the timing later than I expected.
I have had time to think,
have wisdom gifted me despite myself,
learned the perils of haste and anger,
embraced trust and tested love.

Some things I have lost or broken
but even those may be reclaimed,
refashioned in a new light
or way of being, so that nothing is
ever really lost on this earth –
the drop of water that turns to vapour,
or the tyrant's fallen monument
used for builder's sand.

The Muse that guides us is shy,
unsure of how to tell us of our fates,
sighs when we fall and bleed
against walls we have built around
ourselves. Can she now
be trusted to help
find the way when storms begin?

Now I have the sun shining on my back
not glaring in my eyes; the morning
gardens full of birdsong; the pools blue
in the afternoon; marble floors;
rich local wines and in the evening,
the boats motionless
at the port while further out
the bigger shadowy ships
beckon in the breeze.

Down

Autumn comes down
in a million pieces –
spotted, twisted, folded, flattened;
in a hundred vagaries
of green, yellow, orange, wine.

Autumn comes down
under heaven's grey-blue bowl,
spreads light of melted amber
over fields in a light-blue haze
holding in the breath
of a long afternoon.

Autumn comes down
in the silent vortex between seasons,
bearing rich gifts unaccepted,
with all its own frustrated maelstrom
sinking down.

Shadow Walker

I have felt your presence
on wintry evenings,
sensed the shape of your head,
the line of your fragile body.

But I do not know the colour
of your eyes, touch of your skin,
or the tracery of your smiles and sighs.

Like a lake dweller of old,
I feel my way for the path
below the dark surface
lest one slip reveals my secret.

Linger in the shadows a while longer
for I cannot bear
the thought of your coming.